Farmers and Ranchers Care about their Animals!

by
Dan Yunk

Grandma, Addie and I are going out on the porch to play school.

We're taking along our stuffed animals and babies.

We're the students.

2

Would you be our teacher?

I'd like that, Kailey. I want to teach you some more things about agriculture, Grandma replied.

Agriculture is kind of a big word but to me it all comes down to growing crops and raising animals.

Today, our lesson is about raising animals.

Farmers and ranchers have always taken care of their animals.

They take care of them because they enjoy it and because it is the right thing to do.

The safety and well-being of their animals is important to farmers and ranchers.

By making sure their livestock have enough food, water and proper medical care, farmers and ranchers protect their animals' health.

This care for their animals takes place every day of the year.

Rain or shine. Hot or cold.

Farmers realize if they take care of their animals, people like us will have safe products to eat.

Plus, farmers' families eat and use the same animal products we do. It only makes sense they want them to be the best quality.

Good care equals quality food and animal products.

Grandma, do you think Addie will ever know as much about agriculture as you and I know? Kailey asked.

I bet she will, Kailey.

She'll learn more about agriculture just like you have, plus how important it is to us no matter where we live.

She'll also come to understand and appreciate how much our farmers care about their land, the water and their animals!